DEVELOPING YOUR CRITICAL THINKING SKILLS

CONFRONTING YOUR ASSUMPTIONS

Assumptions aren't inherently bad. They're necessary to help us make sense of our world. Our brains are bombarded with so much information we simply couldn't function if we didn't each have some basic premises to work from. That said, the critical thinker knows assumptions can get in the way of rational decision making. In this course, you'll learn how to use questions to identify and check assumptions, distinguish relevant facts from opinion, and seek perspectives from others in managing assumptions.

UNDERSTANDING ASSUMPTIONS

Everyone makes assumptions, and most of the time making assumptions is helpful when you're unsure of something of minor importance. But when thinking critically, it's important to recognize assumptions, the conclusions you and others may jump to, to separate fact from fiction. But what exactly is an assumption. An assumption is a thought or a statement that presents itself as true, but without any proof to back it up. Most of the time, we don't even realize we're assuming things because they appear self-evident to us. Some assumptions are justified, but many aren't. The only way to know for sure is to examine them, asking the right questions. But in order to do that you first have to recognize when assumptions are made.

Say, you run into a former colleague while out shopping, when you ask how his new job is going he cuts you off and says he has to go. You might assume he's having a tough time at work and doesn't want to talk about it. Or if you're feeling sensitive, you might think he doesn't enjoy your company. In either case, the evidence is hardly conclusive. All you have to go on is his behavior during a very short interaction. He may have been distracted by needing to get somewhere urgently or perhaps something upset him recently and he still felt upset, but was uncomfortable showing it. Without evidence you make an assumption. In many cases, assumptions are formed unconsciously. And most often people remain unaware of this until something contradicts them. For example, say you're out at a restaurant and see a man and woman having supper together. You may immediately without realizing it assume they're a couple. It might surprise you to learn they're actually siblings, but unless that was somehow made apparent you would leave the restaurant none the wiser. Sometimes people make fair or reasonable assumptions based on their past experiences or knowledge. But are your assumptions justified. Suppose your car got broken into twice on the same street in a short period of time you would be justified in assuming it's not safe to park there. There's a strong chance anyone in the same position as you would make the same assumption. But you may have just had some really rotten luck. Perhaps there haven't been any other break-ins in that area for several years. It may even have been the same person, but who has since been arrested. Without evidence you don't have any way of knowing for sure.

Recognizing assumptions, your own or those of others around you isn't just occasionally useful, it's the crucial first step in critical thinking.

THE ROLE OF ASSUMPTIONS IN CRITICAL THINKING

Whether personal or related to business, we make decisions constantly, some of which rely on inferences we make. But decisions can be costly if they're not properly thought through. If your thinking depends on assumption, stop and take the time to check its accuracy for the sake of the decision you're making. Checking the validity of assumptions means asking questions. Is it true, is it relevant, what do others think. Suppose you're traveling, you assume walking around this new city at night is unsafe. Your assumption may or may not be correct, but it determines when and whether you decide to go sightseeing. Or perhaps it's perfectly safe. How can you stay safe? The point is you can't be sure. You need to find out the truth and relevance of your assumption. Find out what others think. Fact-check your assumption. Is this assumption true? Take a data-driven approach. Seek out evidence.

Consider this example. Your company wants to cut down on shipping costs. On advice from the marketing team, management decides to charge a shipping fee for orders below $100. Their assumption is that implementing a shipping fee will motivate customers to avoid paying it by spending more than $100. But is that true. Get the facts. Ask marketing for proof that supports their claim. Perhaps they have convincing market trends analysis or evidence of other successful implementations in similar lines of business. The point is that without proof it is merely an assumption that customers will behave that way. Truth isn't the only factor, however. You should also question the relevance of a statement or opinion. An assumption, after all, can be based in fact but still not be meaningful.

Let's say the new shipping fee does motivate customers to spend more on their orders. But what if overall sales revenue actually decreases. Customers might only place larger orders now and then, and end up buying less over time. If the company pays a flat rate for shipping it would then struggle even more to cover its costs. In this case, the initial assumption that a shipping fee will increase the amount customers spend per order becomes irrelevant to the underlying need.

Finally, when testing an assumption, it's a good idea to reach out to others. Do they share your assumptions or have some of their own? If so, why. Ask them. Returning to the shipping fees example, the company could create an online survey to get valuable feedback from customers on the subject. Or they could approach other marketing consultants for an external opinion. No one can avoid making assumptions. They're a fundamental part of everyone's mental makeup, but you can look out for them and question them. In fact, you can't call yourself a critical thinker without examining your own assumptions.

DISTINGUISHING FACTS FROM OPINIONS

Assumptions are statements that are presented as true without offering any proof to back them up. Once you've clearly identified an assumption and asked some initial questions about them, you need to dig a little deeper to gauge their veracity. Broadly speaking, assumptions fall into one of three categories, fact-based, opinion-based, and projection- based. When you spot an assumption it's a good idea to classify it. Knowing the type of assumption, you're dealing with makes it easier to challenge. Assumptions based on facts are statements that stand on their own regardless of who holds them. They are the simplest to deal with because they are either true or false.

For example, there can be no confusion about the current exchange rate between the dollar and the euro. It can be objectively verified leaving no room for debate. The rate may change over time, but whatever its current rate it can be fixed for that specific period. It is a fact. Assumptions based on opinions are tricky because they reflect a person's preferences, values, or feelings. In other words, they're subjective. It can be a tad annoying when we're challenged on a matter of fact. Most people don't like having their personal opinions put under the microscope. At work, when things get difficult it's often because someone's opinion-based assumption has been challenged. For example, you may assume that people in the office are in bad moods because it has been raining all week. While it may be a verifiable fact that it has rained all week, your assumption that this has put everyone in a bad mood is based on an opinion. Rainy days spoil your mood, so they must spoil everyone's. This is a fallacy. Many people like rainy days. So, their bad moods, if they exist at all may well be attributable to something else entirely.

Then finally, projection-based assumptions are opinions about the future. Say your company has just hired a new project manager for a software development team. If you had a really difficult time working under the previous manager, you may assume work conditions are bound to improve. Of course, there may be others on your team who really liked the previous manager. Their outlook might not be so positive regarding the change. In either case, they're making assumptions. Projecting into the future based purely on personal subjective experience. Business requires setting aside assumptions and seeing past personal opinions and baseless projections. It isn't always easy, but critical thinkers need to challenge assumptions of all types.

GUARDING AGAINST FAULTY ASSUMPTIONS

The critical thinker is always asking questions, and never more so than when assumptions are involved. Carefully unpacking and questioning your own thought process allows you to root out faulty assumptions. Not doing so leads to making poor judgment calls with serious consequences in the workplace. When examining assumptions the first thing to ask is always, does this assumption make sense, if not toss it. If it does, ask, is it clear and unambiguous. Ask if there's any proof around the assumption to support it. If there is associated data that supports it, check that it's sufficient and directly related. Is there data I can use to help prove or bolster my case? And ask yourself, can the assumption be looked at in another way. Is it open to personal interpretation? If there are different ways to interpret your assumption or the data to support it, explore them.

Say, you're hosting a seminar and made the assumption it would be best to rent a small venue in which to host it. You're basing this on the fact that only 12 people signed up, and your opinion that the seminar won't be successful in a medium to large-sized venue with only 12 participants. When you tie those two assumptions together you could make the projection that renting a smaller space will create a more intimate environment and make the seminar more successful. Or you could project that getting more people to attend will make it more successful by providing more diverse input. Are you going to be happy with a smaller group and get a smaller space? Or are you going to rent a bigger place and try to beef up enrollment? This requires good critical thinking about your assumptions. They inform your decisions and ultimately dictate which direction you take.

Avoiding faulty assumptions requires analyzing the assumptions you're making about your business situations and asking questions to test their credibility. Does it make sense to say that more people will make the seminar better? Maybe the subject matter lends itself to an intimate setup with a smaller group. What evidence is there to suggest that 12 people aren't enough? Perhaps previous seminars with larger groups had a better atmosphere, or maybe smaller groups never picked up any momentum. Is it clear what success means in this situation? If it's a matter of profitability, then more people is definitely the most successful route. But maybe there's a different way of looking at it. Perhaps success is more about the quality of the experience and how inspiring it is. In that case, the number of participants might be irrelevant to the seminar's success.

Remember, the critical thinker is always asking questions, and never more so than when assumptions are involved.

CHECKING ASSUMPTIONS WITH OTHERS

A key factor in thinking critically is challenging your assumptions by seeking out other people's perspectives to ensure you remain objective. You may think that asking for other people's opinions might lead to trouble since their point of view is likely based on their own and probably different assumptions. But actually, it doesn't matter. If your goal is to make a sound business decision it can only be helpful to discover the assumptions of everyone involved, and to see what, if any, evidence there is to support them. And remember, asking around doesn't mean you have to change your mind or let go of your own assumptions. But at least hear what other people have to say. In fact, it's really valuable to ask for other people's perspectives throughout the whole critical thinking process.

To help keep feedback focused, ask specific questions. Present your assumption and ask, "What do you think about that? Have you ever experienced that? Is there some other assumption I'm neglecting to consider? How do you think this will play out in this situation? How do you think this assumption will impact the decision I'm trying to make?" Ask open-ended questions. Then really listen to what people have to say. It's easy to fall into the trap of only getting perspectives from people who are likely to agree with you. Avoid it. It's also tempting to find other perspectives within your own circle at work. Asking your colleagues and coworkers is fine, but it's better to go outside of your immediate circle, even outside of your company. Go online; ask face to face, post on your blog. Try to get as broad a perspective as possible from other people.

For example, let's say your assumption is that people prefer to buy products online. To get other perspectives, you would ask people who are big online shoppers what they prefer about shopping in this way. And you'd ask people who like to go shop in stores why they favor that. It would also be worthwhile asking people who don't do a lot of shopping why that is. You may find some really valuable data that defeats your assumption that people like to shop online. Perhaps people are generally trying to shop less in general. In the process of speaking to others they're likely to share their assumptions with you.

When checking the validity of these, ask open-ended questions to help you get to the bottom of their thinking. Never be afraid to ask for input, why do you think that is a simple but powerful question. Test assumptions, your own and those of others. Always seek to get a wide range of perspectives on questionable issues and be sure to test the further assumptions that underlie them. After all, if we could easily see the flaws in our own assumptions then we wouldn't hold them in the first place.

EXERCISE: COMING TO TERMS WITH ASSUMPTIONS

In this exercise, you need to be able to recognize and challenge assumptions appropriately. In this exercise, you'll demonstrate that you can
- identify assumptions when they occur
- distinguish between facts, opinions, and projections, and
- guard against faulty assumptions and get alternative viewpoints to check their validity

Question
Which statements accurately describe assumptions?
Options:
1. They are presented as truth without proof 2. They are often made unknowingly
3. They are sometimes warranted
4. They help strengthen an argument
5. They are necessary for critical thinking Answer

Option 1: This is a correct option. An assumption is a thought or statement that isn't supported by evidence or rational argument.

Option 2: This is a correct option. Oftentimes we don't realize we're making an assumption because it's presented as an unquestionable truth.

Option 3: This is a correct option. Assumptions are sometimes justified. They may be reasonable based on what you've experienced in the past.

Option 4: *This is an incorrect option. A strong argument is based on reliable facts and logic. An assumption is an unsupported claim, such as an opinion.*

Option 5: *This is an incorrect option. Critical thinking is used for objective analysis, whereas an assumption is a subjective claim.*

Question

You applied internally for a management position two weeks ago but still haven't received feedback. You feel it's because you lack experience.

Which questions should you ask to check your assumptions?

Options:
1. What evidence is there to suggest I don't have the relevant experience?
2. Is experience an important factor in deciding who gets the job?
3. What do my colleagues think is the reason for me not having received feedback yet?
4. How can I improve my resume?
5. What other positions are available that require less experience?

Answer

Option 1: *This is a correct option. Check whether your assumption is true. Evaluate your career experience and consider whether it has prepared you for the management position.*

Option 2: *This is a correct option. Check whether your assumption is relevant. Perhaps qualifications are more important for the position than experience.*

Option 3: *This is a correct option. Asking what other people think is a great way to test whether an assumption is valid.*

Option 4: *This is an incorrect option. The need to improve your resume is based on your assumption that you lack experience. It doesn't help evaluate the assumption.*

Option 5: *This is an incorrect option. The motivation for looking for another position is based on your assumption that you lack experience. It won't help determine whether the assumption is well founded.*

Question
Sales for your new range of juicers have been disappointing. You think it's due to their unfashionable aesthetics.
Match each assumption to its category. Categories may have more than one match.
Options:
A. The juicer market is already saturated
B. Demand for the product was overestimated
C. 90% of sales revenues come from sales of other household appliances D. The company needs to focus on downsizing the product line
E. The least profitable products will be eliminated
Targets:
1. Facts
2. Opinions 3. Projections
Answer
An assumption based on a fact has data that is clear, specific, and verifiable. Stating where 90% of company sales come from is something that can be checked and proven to be either true or false.

Your claims that the market for juicing appliances is saturated, product demand was overestimated, and the company should downsize its product range are all personal opinions that convey how you feel about the situation. They are also subjective points of view that are not supported by evidence.

A projection is a type of opinion that predicts. For example, you predict that in downsizing the company's product range, the more unprofitable products, such as the line of juicers, will be removed.

Question
Which questions should you ask to determine whether an assumption is defective?
Options:
1. Is the meaning of the assumption clear?
2. Does the assumption make sense?
3. Is there any evidence to support the assumption? 4. Do my col-

leagues hold the same assumption?

5. How strongly do I feel about the assumption?

Answer

Option 1: *This is a correct option. If the meaning is unclear or ambiguous then the assumption is unsuitable for the purposes of critical thinking.*

Option 2: *This is a correct option. The first thing to check is whether the assumption actually makes sense. For example, if it isn't practical, then there's no point in evaluating it further.*

Option 3: *This is a correct option. Always check the facts. If there isn't enough information to back the claim up, then it can't be reliable.*

Option 4: *This is an incorrect option. It isn't relevant who holds the assumption. Just because everyone believes it, doesn't make it true. Focus on the merits of the assumption itself.*

Option 5: *This is an incorrect option. Having a strong emotional investment in the assumption can cloud your judgement. Your feelings may be biased or unreasonable.*

Question

Your company's new tablet range is set to launch next week but you're behind schedule. You feel the testing phase can be reduced to save time. You check with your team.

Which questions should you ask?

Options:
1. Have you ever cut down testing time to meet a software release deadline?
2. How could this decision affect the success of the new tablet range?
3. Do you think it's a good idea to reduce the testing phase in favor of launching on schedule?
4. How much time should we cut from the testing phase?
5. What plans should we put in place to address software bugs post launch?

Answer

Option 1: *This is a correct option. Asking others if they've had similar experiences is a great way to avoid repeating past mistakes.*

Option 2: *This is a correct option. Asking your team how they think things will play out helps ensure you take all unwelcome consequences into consideration.*

Option 3: *This is a correct option. Asking what your team thinks will help uncover other assumptions and any evidence there is to support them.*

Option 4: *This is an incorrect option. This question doesn't help evaluate your assumption. Instead, it's based on the assumption being the best solution.*

Option 5: *This is an incorrect option. This question is based on your proposed solution. But you should find out whether it's the right one first.*

INVESTIGATING ARGUMENTS

Arguments are an expected part of the critical-thinking process. Without them, you can't make well thought-out decisions or reach logical conclusions. You regularly make arguments because you want to make a point or move an issue forward. Your ability to recognize and evaluate their validity determines your aptitude for thinking critically.

In this course, you'll learn how to identify arguments, recognize persuasion techniques, explore arguments for accuracy, precision, and logic, and make strong arguments of your own.

SPOTTING AN ARGUMENT

Much of day-to-day life involves making and navigating arguments. Being able to spot one is an essential building block of critical thinking. In everyday language an argument is a disagreement between people or a lawyer statement in court. The term seems a little intimidating, hostile even. But in critical thinking terms, an argument is a positive thing. It's simply a statement that includes reasons for accepting a conclusion.

When you're thinking critically, you and others will make arguments for or against something. You'll use them to make a point or to bring a decision or a conclusion closer to being real. Ideally an argument should be accurate, precise, logical, and free of bias or persuasion. Typically, an argument has two parts. Some rationale followed by a conclusive statement.

For example, a project team might argue that because of losing a key member, they can't meet a project deadline. That's something you've probably heard before. Now consider it from an argument perspective. Is it accurate that that person really was a key player? And is it logical that by losing one member the team won't be able to meet the project deadline? Also consider bias and persuasion.

Is the team just trying to guilt trip their manager into cutting them some slack to cover the fact that they've gone off schedule? Extending the deadline might be fair, but it would still be wise to think about the argument itself. Consider the impact the decision might have on factors like customers and cost. A good way to spot an argument is to check for terms like since, therefore, or as a result.

These let you know the speaker is using a seemingly rational and conclusive statement to build an argument. For example, the statement, our competitor has reduced their prices, therefore we need to match that contains a seemingly obvious fact and a conclusive statement. It's the critical thinker's job to ensure one leads logically to the other. Don't confuse an argument with an assumption.

An argument is meant to convince you of something, whereas an assumption isn't necessarily trying to convince you of anything. If I make the assumption that meetings are more productive when there's an agenda, that's what I assume. But if I say meetings are more productive when there's an agenda, therefore we should only have meetings when there's an agenda. That's an argument. I'm making a statement.

And then I'm giving you a conclusive statement associated with it. There's also a difference between stating an opinion and making an argument. If your boss tells you her favorite color is red, that's an opinion. If she tells you her favorite color is red therefore the new product packaging should be red, that's an argument. You can't realistically take a position against other people's opinions, but their arguments are fair game and require critical thinking.

JUDGING AN ARGUMENT

Simply recognizing an argument when you hear one or make one is not in itself critical thinking. Evaluating the argument's reasoning and judging whether or not it leads logically to some conclusive point, that's critical thinking. If you want to determine whether an argument is accurate, precise, and logical, the best place to start is to ask questions. Ask where the data came from, and what evidence there is behind it.

And take the time and effort to find out what other people think about it. Also question whether you could be more specific. Could you provide additional detail, and check within yourself. Am I accepting this argument as accurate, precise, and logical because it holds up to scrutiny? Or is it because the person is so persuasive that it sounds like something I should agree with? For example, if somebody says to you the market is down at the moment, so it's a good time to buy stock.

You might think, oh that's right. I've heard it's a good time to buy stock. In some situations that argument may be accurate, but you should still question whether it's relevant to your current circumstances. And you should also consider how the person who's delivering the argument may be influencing your perception. If it was a Wall Street stockbroker for instance, you might be more easily persuaded or biased to believe that argument.

You need to exercise judgment. So what are the criteria by which you should judge an argument? There are five basic criteria to take into account. You can think of them in terms of questions you should ask yourself. Every time you encounter an argument first ask is the argument and its supporting data clear? Next is the supporting data actually relevant to the argument? Is there sufficient data to support the conclusion?

Does the argument's reasoning lead logically to its conclusion? And finally is the argument based on reason and is it objective? Or does it merely appeal to biases and emotions? Spotting a good argument takes practice. It's easy to confuse what you feel with what you think. But once you get the hang of it, it becomes second nature, and critical thinking becomes a standard tool.

OVERCOMING LOGICAL FALLACIES

Good business arguments are logical and present valid reasons for their conclusions. But when thinking about an argument in terms of logic watch out for so-called fallacies. There are five common logical fallacies. The first three to look at happen when the information that's available is misinterpreted. You're certainly familiar with the first "Overgeneralizing". This happens when someone argues that something is true in general merely because it's true in a particular case.

You might say I've been watching how some of our end users reacted to our latest product for two days. It's obvious it won't be successful. That's generalizing before there is enough evidence to back the argument up. The next major fallacy to avoid is the "False Dichotomy". A Dichotomy is a contrast or division between two different options. A False Dichotomy is an assumption where there are only two options.

It's used to force agreement by reducing an argument to only two choices, when in fact there are other options. It can also imply that two situations are mutually exclusive when they're not. Someone might say well of course as a business we can engage in socially conscious activities in the community but it'll affect our productivity. There's no doubt about that. It's a false dichotomy because it implies you can't be involved in community projects, and still maintain high levels of productivity.

Then there's the fallacy of Incorrect Association also called "Post Hoc Ergo Propter Hoc". This fallacy argues that because two events happened in sequence the first must have caused the second. For example our sales went down in the holiday season, therefore it's safe to assume the holidays are the cause. It may be true, but it's a poor argument because the drop in sales could have been caused by any number of other variables.

The next two fallacies relate directly to people. The first is called "The Argument From Authority". We've all fallen victim to this at one time or another. It happens when someone bases an argument on their or someone else's experience or expertise in a field. Your boss might say I've been working in IT for twenty years and I'm telling you it's time to upgrade our servers.

Just because someone holds a senior position or is regarded as an expert on a particular subject doesn't necessarily mean every statement, they make is true. Finally, there is the fallacy of "Arguing Against The Person" or "Ad hominem". It's what happens when you attack a person rather than the argument they're making. For example, someone in accounting might say we shouldn't store files on the SharePoint site just because IT says so.

storing files in a particular location. By using critical thinking to spot logical fallacies in arguments, you make better decisions and can avoid using them yourself.

FACING PERSUASIVE TACTICS

An argument can appear to make perfect sense at first glance. But on closer inspection you find it appeals to your emotions or personal biases not logic. As a critical thinker you need to be mindful of these traps and carefully avoid them. How can an unsound argument be persuasive? Emotion often gets in the way of critical thinking. You can go along with an argument because it's easier to do so, because you wanted to be true or because it confirms your own opinion or beliefs.

Persuasive techniques draw on our emotions and use them against us. Be vigilant and keep your emotions in check when thinking critically. It's okay to go with your feelings when it's appropriate but recognize when your emotions are getting in the way of logical thinking. Understand how a persuasive technique works to strengthen the argument. Persuasive techniques can get your audience to agree with you, but they aren't good methods to use in business arguments.

They promote muddy thinking. Think about these four key persuasive techniques. The first is 'Asserting Rightness'. This is no more complicated than it sounds. Some people will simply look you in the eye and declare repeatedly that they're right and you are wrong. Their confidence alone can be persuasive. Assertion of rightness is often backed up by some claim to authority. I was in the meeting and you weren't, for example.

The second technique is 'Asserting Priorities'. This happens when you claim that what you want is the most important factor. For example, someone may respond to your argument with, that may be true, but what matters here is profit. That's asserting priority. It doesn't explain why profits are more important. Your argument may be perfectly sound. And referring to some outside issue does nothing to undermine it.

The third persuasive technique involves 'Reframing Criteria'. This happens when someone plays down factors that don't suit their argument and amplifies those that do. It's good salesmanship but it isn't good critical thinking. Finally, we have the technique of sowing doubt. This is all about negativity and knocking an argument without saying anything substantial about it. A typical example is the empty statement, 'I don't know how you could possibly think that'.

Maintain confidence when someone is bad mouthing your argument. Stay calm and stick to the facts. There are four additional persuasive techniques to look out for. Two of them relate to research. The first happens when someone undermines research that doesn't support their argument. The second is when they deliberately misquote existing research to suit their argument.

Another technique is to change the rules during an argument to suit your case, sometimes called moving the goalposts. It's similar to strategic forgetting, conveniently forgetting facts that disprove an argument. Be vigilant of these tactics and remember that a sound argument doesn't rely on cheap tricks. It stands on its own merits.

PREPARING YOUR ARGUMENT

The goal of an argument is to present a proposition that's both logical and convincing. Building and presenting a sound, solid argument is something that requires preparation. When preparing an argument remember that you're trying to convince somebody to move in a particular direction or reach a particular conclusion. Always assume they are a critical thinker.

That means building an argument that's held together by accurate facts and sound logic, not bias and persuasion. Ask yourself, 'Do I have enough evidence to support my argument'? Is it the right evidence? Is it clear? Is it relevant? Is it objective? Does my argument have a logical flow that makes sense? These are the things to focus your efforts on when preparing to sway someone's point of view.

If the answer to any of these questions is no, you have more work in preparation to do. Being properly prepared to deliver your argument holds a number of benefits for you. First you'll be comfortable knowing you have all the data and evidence you need to support your argument. Second, your argument will be more convincing. A well-thought through argument is clear, and speaks for itself. You won't have to force it, skirt nervously around holes in your line of thinking or grasp for answers if questioned.

And finally, you'll feel more confident in your claim. There won't be any need to bend facts or win people over by resorting to persuasive tactics. A well-reasoned, thoughtfully delivered argument is a thing of beauty. Be thorough and give your argument all the attention and preparation it deserves.

MAKING A GOOD ARGUMENT

The point of arguing is to convince someone to acknowledge your point of view. To do that, you need a strong argument. There are four criteria that must be met when constructing a strong argument. Before arguing your case, it's a good idea to check whether you've adequately met each one. The first requirement is to strip the argument of assumptions, beliefs, opinions, and reasons that aren't strictly rational.

If you can't get rid of them all, at least make sure to flag them using phrases like, I'm making an assumption here or in my personal opinion. It's better to point out any flaws in your argument than to have someone else do it for you. Next make sure there are strong reasons for reaching your conclusion. Any reasonable person should arrive at the same outcome, given the facts and following sound logic.

Check that your reasoning is rock solid, and tie it to your conclusion using words like because, since and therefore. Third avoid appeals to emotion and bias, and any other persuasive techniques that don't follow naturally from the evidence. Show confidence in your logic but make sure your confidence is built on a firm foundation. Finally, it's crucial that you use good communication skills. The best arguments are clear and concise.

Remember to accept and answer questions, challenges, and feedback graciously. Show respect for other viewpoints even when you disagree. Consider an example that illustrates the application of these criteria. Marketing is appealing to management to develop and launch an eco-friendly version of the product. They claim it will increase revenue by opening the door to eco-conscious consumers. They don't base this on an assumption about what consumers want.

Instead they rely on accurate market research data showing that millennial customers are more concerned with the environmental impact of products than price, convenience or any other factor. With the help of the finance department, they also provide a detailed breakdown of the associated product development costs. It indicates that the product will earn acceptable margins.

Their approach doesn't appeal to the company's moral obligations as a manufacturer or to a sentimental sense of responsibility and is communicated using the right channels. And that sounds like a great argument to me. Before presenting an argument, check that it meets each of the four key criteria. Consider your argument from all angles. Are you missing something?

Is there another way of interpreting the information? Once your argument flows naturally to its conclusion, present it clearly, and concisely, and have faith in the power of reason and critical thinking.

EXERCISE: IDENTIFYING AND GENERATING ARGUMENTS

In this exercise, you need to be able to judge arguments and recognize strategies for making strong arguments so you can ensure your decisions are well thought out.

In this exercise, you'll demonstrate that you can
- identify and evaluate arguments
- recognize logic problems and persuasion techniques in an argument
- recognize the value of preparation, and
- choose the best argument to support a conclusion

Question

The lead safety officer at your company, a manufacturer of specialist metal tools, sends out minutes from the monthly safety meeting.

Which statements from the minutes are arguments?

Options:
1. "Fire drills are meant to take place this week. I'll be in contact with the department to let them know."
2. "I think we need to actually dedicate an individual to spearhead the workplace safety inspections this year."
3. "I noticed on three occasions in the last week that

DEVELOPING YOUR CRITICAL THINKING SKILLS

machinists were not adhering to safety standards, so I think it's imperative that we set up refresher hazard training to all floor personnel."
4. "The carriage on the lathe in room 5 is not moving properly. Since this can potentially cause injury, we need to stop using this machine and organize a full service."

Answer

Option 1: *This is an incorrect option. It is simply a fact that fire drills are to take place. There is no assumption or conclusion.*

Option 2: *This is an incorrect option. Although a conclusion seems to have been made, there is no assumption or data to suggest why this is. Without information to support it, it is simply an opinion.*

Option 3: *This is a correct option. There is a clear argument here. The conclusion – that hazard training needs to be set up – is supported by the assumption that floor staff are not aware of safety standards, which is based on observations.*

Option 4: *This is a correct option. You can recognize arguments by keywords like "since." The conclusion that the machine is potentially dangerous and needs to be serviced is based on the reason that the carriage is not functioning properly.*

Question
Which questions should you ask when assessing an argument?
Options:
1. Is the data supporting the argument relevant?
2. Does the argument's reasoning lead logically to the conclusion?
3. Is the argument based on reason or emotion?
4. Is the argument in line with my beliefs?
5. How educated is the person delivering the argument?
6. Is there enough information to support the conclusion?
7. Are the argument and the data it's based on clear?

Answer

Option 1: *This is a correct option. If the facts don't relate to the argument, then it hasn't been carefully thought through.*

Option 2: *This is a correct option. An argument's conclusion should flow naturally from its reasoning. If not, the evidence may be inconclu-*

sive or lead to a different conclusion.

Option 3: This is a correct option. A sound argument is based on rational thought processes. It doesn't rely on people's preconceived opinions or feelings.

Option 4: This is an incorrect option. An argument may ring true with your beliefs but still be weak and unreasonable.

Option 5: This is an incorrect option. An argument should be judged on its own terms, not according to the person who presents it.

Option 6: This is a correct option. Without sufficient data, the conclusion becomes less reliable. Ideally, you want a wide range of relevant data to strengthen your conclusion.

Option 7: This is a correct option. A strong argument is clear and concise, with an unambiguous meaning. The evidence it's based on also needs to be clear so that it's easy to understand how the argument makes sense of it.

Question
Match each statement to the category of logical fallacy it relates to.

Options:
1. "Ed agrees with me and he's handled bigger projects successfully."
2. "I know sales were bad last year, but we'll get a raise. We've always gotten them before."
3. "I know it's pricey, but if we don't get new software, we'll lose our reputation as market leaders."
4. "Since the new guy arrived, the Internet's been slow. He must be downloading media."
5. E. "Why should we listen to you? You've only worked here two months."

Targets:
1. Argument from authority
2. Overgeneralizing
3. False dichotomy
4. Incorrect association
5. Arguing against the person

Answer

An argument from authority is when the proponent uses their or someone else's experience or expertise in a field to lend credibility to their opinion, such as arguing that someone who's been successful on other projects agrees with them.

Overgeneralizing occurs when someone makes a general claim based on only a few facts, such as saying that employees will get a salary increase because they always have in the past.

A false dichotomy is a situation in which two alternatives are presented as the only options available when in fact there are others – for example, arguing that you can get new software or lose your reputation.

Also called post hoc ergo propter hoc or after, therefore, because this is the fallacy of an incorrect association. Just because events x and y both happened – for example, a new employee and decreased Internet speed – doesn't necessarily mean that one caused the other.

Also called argument ad hominem, this is the fallacy whereby you attack a person rather than the argument they are making.

Question

Match each statement to the corresponding persuasion technique.

Options:
1. "My interpretation is accurate. You're just not looking at it from the right perspective."
2. "That's all very well, but remember it always comes down to sales figures in this business."
3. "I know it doesn't have as many features as last year's model, but think of how much cheaper it will be to manufacture!"
4. "Don't you see how violently those colors clash? Are you sure you have an eye for design?"

Targets:
1. Asserting rightness 2. Asserting priorities 3. Reframing criteria 4. Sowing doubt

Answer

Asserting rightness is confidently saying that you're right and the other person's perspective is wrong. It's sometimes paired with an assertion of special knowledge, authority, or expertise.

When someone asserts priorities, they claim that what they want is more important than the argument being made against them – for example, by saying a business is all about sales figures.

Reframing criteria happens when someone plays down those criteria that don't support their cause and highlights those that do – for example, by downplaying reduced features by highlighting reduced manufacturing costs.

Sowing doubt is a technique where you take advantage of some small doubt to create bigger doubts – for example, by asking someone if they're sure they have the skills they claim to have.

Question

What are the advantages of preparing properly for an argument?

Options:

1. You will have all the available evidence to support your argument
2. Your delivery will be convincing
3. You will feel confident about persuading people because you will have your facts straight
4. You will know which facts to downplay
5. You can practice techniques of persuasion that suit your argument

Answer

Option 1: This is a correct option. Being properly prepared means, you will be organized and be able to back up your claims with information you've gathered.

Option 2: This is a correct option. When you carefully think an argument through, you can present it clearly and let it speak for itself.

Option 3: This is a correct option. Preparing for an argument is laying the groundwork. When it comes time to present it, you will be familiar with all the evidence and feel calm and confident in your reasoning.

Option 4: This is an incorrect option. A well-prepared argument makes sense of all the evidence and presents it fairly. If you have to avoid

holes in your line of thinking, then you may be unprepared.
Option 5: *This is an incorrect option. There won't be any need to bend facts or win people over by resorting to persuasive tactics.*

Question
After extensive research, you believe it's time for your company to start replacing its manual machines with automated machines, so you pitch it to your CFO.
Which statement is the best argument?
Options:
1. "You really have to see some of these machines to believe them. The design possibilities are staggering, and the advantages they could provide will blow you away."
2. "You've got to trust me on this. I know what I'm talking about. And wouldn't it be great to be the only small company in our field that's fully automated? Our competitors will be green with envy!"
3. "There are costs associated with replacing the machinery for sure, but they are far outweighed by the cost savings in terms of person hours in both operation and testing of components. How about I send you a full cost-benefit report?"
4. "I appreciate that there are cost issues around this, but the data really supports the upgrade. The automated machines are 18% more precise than manual machines, and 25% more consistent. And fewer technicians are required to operate them."

Answer
Option 1: *This is an incorrect option. Don't use statements based on emotion. Your CFO may not be that interested in the delights of technology. Present facts and data to enable your CFO to reach the same conclusions as you.*
Option 2: *This is an incorrect option. Avoid persuasive devices, such as appeals to authority and emotions. It may increase the chances of the argument being accepted, but ultimately it lacks clarity. Your CFO will probably be a critical thinker and therefore not take your argu-*

ment seriously.

Option 3: *This is the correct option. Construct an argument using reasons and data that are relevant and really support the conclusion. Data about cost will support your argument in this case, since that's what the CFO is concerned about. It's also good to avoid appealing to emotions and to strip your response of assumptions and irrationality.*

Option 4: *This is an incorrect option. Although data can support your argument, use data that's relevant. The CFO's concern relates to cost, not precision or efficiency, so use data related to cost instead.*

REACHING SOUND CONCLUSIONS

Drawing conclusions is about analyzing, and weighing the information, and sources that support taking action. It's about questions too. You can only be confident that your conclusion is sound when you've closely queried its clarity, accuracy, specificity, relevance, logic, and depth. In this course you will learn how to recognize the critical-thinking activities associated with reaching a sound conclusion. Employ effective questions, use tools to help you conclude findings, and create an action plan for putting conclusions into practice.

ELEMENTS OF A LOGICAL CONCLUSION

A conclusion is a call to action. It should lead to some result or change. Otherwise, it's no more than an intellectual exercise. Of course, rushing into change without having formed a proper conclusion invariably leads to trouble. Due diligence is necessary to come to a logical, actionable conclusion. Critical thinkers never jump to conclusions. The process of reaching a good, sound conclusion isn't linear.

Once you're at the point of drawing a conclusion, rise above the information you've gathered and survey it from an aerial perspective. From there, you can circle around the data, synthesizing, and weighing it, and considering it from different angles. You should be constantly rechecking facts, reweighing evidence, re-examining arguments, and resoliciting input. There are essentially three parts to the process of arriving at a good conclusion.

The first part is identifying the relevant data and evidence. This consists of the central pool of resources you've collected so far, data, information, assumptions you've checked, and arguments that make sense. And as you're about to reach a conclusion or make a decision, you'll circle this pool of resources and take it into consideration. Suppose a company is considering whether to enter market segment A or segment B.

First you pull together data related to say the profitability of A versus B, the growth rate of A versus B, and the revenue size of A versus B, and so on. There's your pool of data. The second part involves synthesizing, and weighing the data and evidence, so that it points to a conclusion. When you synthesize the data, you pull from the pool of collected information and organize it into logical groups, clusters, or categories.

You may use visual tools such as diagrams and charts to aid you in doing this. Next you weigh the data. To do that you'll need to establish criteria that define which information is more or less important. Otherwise, all your data will have the same priority waiting. So for our market segment example, the company might weigh profitability over the size of the revenue. That's their priority.

And then like everything else in critical thinking you're going to want to validate the conclusions you've drawn by asking for other people's perspectives. Ask around and find out if others see things the same way you do. Perhaps some assumptions have crept in that need to be re-examined or maybe not everyone agrees with the way you've synthesized and weighed the data.

Back to our example. This is why you might for instance set up a meeting with key, cross-functional stakeholders to vet your analysis and conclusions. An informed conclusion needs the opinions and validation of others. Remember a well-engineered conclusion isn't suddenly reached in a flash of inspiration. It's carefully nurtured and evolves over time employing a thought-out process.

CONCLUDING WITH QUESTIONS

Asking questions is a major part of critical thinking. Just as you question your assumptions and arguments you must also question your conclusions. By the time you've arrived at a conclusion, you've checked a lot of your information already. But this is really a necessary measure twice, cut once exercise. Be careful to recognize any new assumptions you might be making and question those too.

The questions you need to ask about your conclusions fall under four main headings. The first relates to the source. Here you're asking questions like where did you get your information? Can you trace it back to its various sources? And are those sources reliable? Let's say you're pitching for your company to replace its manual performance review system with a software solution.

You need to check which sources you relied on when deciding the software was a good fit for your business. Ideally this information would have come from discussions between the software experts and the managers currently responsible for conducting the reviews. If not, were your other sources reliable? The next set of questions falls under interpretation. What does your data say? How did you go about processing it?

And is your understanding relevant, accurate and unbiased? So returning to the software solution example. Are the affected managers frustrated with the current review process? Are they genuinely interested in learning how to use the new software effectively? Or are they simply trying to get out of having to go to any extra effort? How did you decide on your interpretation? The third set of questions falls under alternatives.

Here you're asking if there are other ways of understanding the data. Based on the information collected so far, what other conclusions could be drawn? Is there another way of looking at it? Does the data point to your company's performance review system being flawed? Or is the underlying methodology the real problem? Do you really need a whole new system? Or can you make modifications to the old system in order to improve the current process?

Would any reasonable person reach the same understanding? Or might they legitimately differ? And finally consider the implications of the conclusion you're reaching. What are the risks and benefits of acting according to your conclusions? If you make a decision and take a specific course of action, what can you expect to happen? In the case of your proposed software solution, how many software user licenses will you need to purchase?

How much time will it take to implement? And what are the associated costs? Does the vendor provide training? Is there a trial period to run a pilot, reducing the risk of purchasing a product that doesn't scale well. Questioning conclusions is just common sense. But that doesn't mean it can be done casually. The critical thinker adopts a careful and deliberate approach and takes nothing for granted.

VISUALIZING DATA

At the conclusion stage of a critical-thinking process, it's often helpful to create diagrams, illustrations, and other visual aids. Sometimes the best way to draw conclusions is with pen and paper. We live in a world that's very analytical. We base a lot of our decisions on data and analysis. Drawing a conclusion that's based on critical thinking deserves to be depicted. After all, a picture is worth a thousand words.

It can quickly explain how you made sense of the data, and how it leads to your conclusions. And that's very important because you'll typically have to count on others to follow through on your findings and take action on your decisions. They will want to know whether you've looked at all the data, and how well you've made sense of it. If they can see it the same way you do, you'll have a much better chance of getting them on board.

Everyone has been in situations where people go on and on using words and expressions to try and motivate them. But being able to put up a visual aid helps make a powerful impression, and can render the same information far more accessible. Visuals can translate all your findings, research, and thinking into something clear and concise that speaks for itself. This gives you more confidence in the decision you're making, and helps to substantiate the ways in which

it could benefit your team or your company.

So for example using a graph or a chart, you can show just how big a percentage of customers said they wanted one product featured over another in a specific product offering, which features they wanted, and what that means moving forward with respect to the product. It's very important to make things as visual and logical as you can, especially in today's world where so many of those tools are readily at our disposal.

DRAWING CONCLUSIONS USING VISUAL TOOLS

There is a wide range of visual tools available to help you draw and depict your conclusions. Representing your thinking visually is a great way to clarify it for yourself and receive valuable input from others. Verbal description can be open to interpretation. Visualization assures you that your audience sees exactly what you intend them to see. It's a matter of choosing the right tool for showing your specific content.

The first visual tool we will look at is the affinity diagram. It's used for organizing information into common themes or clusters, and then labeling those clusters accordingly. These diagrams are helpful when you're feeling swamped by input. And they're especially effective for showing the relationships between different ideas. Two-by-two matrices are also helpful for visualizing relationships.

A two-by-two matrix is a great tool for comparing alternative options along two dimensions such as cost and quality, or time and effort. It can help you represent relationships between specific elements of a problem or weigh up costs and benefits. Then there are flow diagrams or charts. These are good for detailing logical steps and decision points, showing inputs and outputs, cause and effect.

They are particularly useful for solutions that involve a step-by-step process or illustrating when one action can have multiple independent effects. Mind mapping is another common visual tool. A mind map is convenient for chunking ideas into logical groups and showing the relationships between them. A typical mind map has a core idea at its center with ever finer branches leading away from it.

Finally Fishbone diagrams are used to illustrate how various inputs correlate to produce an output. This is often helpful in analyzing and identifying the causes of a problem which is the first step to finding a solution. It's surprising how often areas for improvement or outright errors can go unnoticed until they are part of a diagram or chart. Your critical thinking will be the better for it.

Taking the time to visualize your conclusion allows you and your audience to examine it graphically where any possible holes and gaps can be found more easily, or conversely visual tools allow you to convince your audience of the validity of your decision. It's right there in front of them.

ACTING ON YOUR THINKING

Critical thinking isn't just an analytical process. It must lead to action. Reaching a conclusion always begs the question now what do we do? Many teams or groups do everything right when considering an issue, but fall at the last hurdle acting on their conclusions. Within any organization the purpose of critical thinking is to make sound decisions typically with significant real- world consequences.

So as a critical thinker you have to be aware of the context in which your conclusions will be put to work. And you must be able to present and communicate your conclusions in a way that engages people, and moves decisions forward. The groundwork of solid arguments and the final conclusions have to translate into an achievable and measurable outcome to prove valuable.

To ensure conclusions are implemented efficiently you need to create an action plan that addresses five key questions. First what is the outcome? In other words if we accept the conclusion then what is it that needs to be done? Let's say the conclusion you've reached is that you need to outsource your customer service functions to an outside vendor, decided.

Next who is accountable? The action plan has to assign responsibilities to various people who will be held accountable for carrying out their tasks. In the case of the customer service outsourcing, the purchasing department would be responsible for researching and selecting the vendor. The HR department will be responsible for implementing a transition plan for existing staff. The head of customer service will be responsible for developing new procedures for the department in light of the outsourcing decision. Having allocated responsibilities, the next two questions to address are interrelated. When will the relevant tasks be completed by, and how will they be completed? The answers to these questions should include a step-by-step process for aligning people, time and money if necessary, to complete the required action.

A realistic schedule will need to be drawn up and it will have to take into account how long each task will take, and how it should be carried out. In our example suppose the project will be broken down into three phases with the final phase completed within nine months. The schedule will need to be adjusted to work around that. And it will need to explain what must be done to reach our goal. Finally, why are we taking this action?

The answer to this should arise from the critical thinking process that created the conclusion. There should be a direct link from the action back to the context of the original issue. Returning to the customer service example perhaps the reason for the move is simply this. It's too expensive for us to operate that function in-house. And we can't provide 24/7 support which our competitors provide.

Reaching a sound conclusion but failing to properly act upon it is like coming up with a great recipe, but never actually cooking anything. Well it's called critical thinking. Never forget that its final purpose involves action.

EXERCISE: DRAWING CONCLUSIONS

The way you go about reaching a conclusion is pivotal because it determines the actions you will take moving forward. In this exercise, you'll demonstrate that you recognize how to draw sound conclusions and how to go about putting them into practice.

In this exercise, you'll demonstrate that you can

- understand how to use critical thinking to reach a sound conclusion
- double check your conclusions through questioning
- use visualization techniques to help confirm the logic of your conclusions, and
- complete the critical thinking cycle by formulating a plan of action

Question

Having completed extensive research for the launch of a new agricultural product, you must now make sense of the data.

What critical thinking activities should you use to help draw your conclusions?

Options:
1. Decide which data and evidence is most relevant to the product's success
2. Weed out any input that clashes with the business objectives for the product
3. Weigh all the evidence from all the sources by using criteria that assigns more or less importance to different facts

    4. Validate your findings with farmers and others in the field to get their perspectives
    5. Use visual tools to shape the data to suit your needs

Answer

Option 1: *This is a correct option. The first step is to identify the information most valuable for drawing your conclusions. This is the central pool of resources you'll take into consideration when making a decision.*

Option 2: *This is an incorrect option. The critical thinking process demands that you take input, opinions, and information from as wide a range of people and sources as possible.*

Option 3: *This is a correct option. It is important to recognize which pieces of information are more or less important to the conclusion-drawing process in order to achieve the right balance.*

Option 4: *This is a correct option. Taking other people's perspectives into consideration will reveal whether there are other ways of interpreting the data. It will also help identify anything you've missed or based on unreliable assumptions.*

Option 5: *This is an incorrect option. The purpose of critical thinking is to discover what the data shows from an objective point of view. Your conclusions need to be based on an accurate and impartial interpretation.*

Question

Having struggled to attract talented young coders, you've decided to rebrand your software company to appeal to a younger market.

Which questions should you ask to ensure this is the right approach?

Options:
    1. Where did the information I'm basing this rebranding decision on come from and is it reliable?
    2. What are the costs associated with the rebranding and are the potential benefits worthwhile?
    3. Is the company's image the real issue or is it actually the office culture and work conditions?

4. Does the business really need younger programmers to be innovative and successful?
5. What will our competitors think of the rebranding exercise?
6. Which marketing and design company should I choose to do the rebranding?

Answer

Option 1: This is a correct option. Always try to trace your information back to its sources and check whether they're trustworthy. Your decision can only be as good as the information you're basing it on.

Option 2: This is a correct option. Always think about what will happen if you take a specific course of action. Follow your thinking through to take all risks and benefits into consideration.

Option 3: This is a correct option. Check whether there are other ways of interpreting the data that you might have missed. It may well lead to more than one possible conclusion.

Option 4: This is a correct option. Be sure to check your understanding of the data. Although the sources may show your company doesn't appeal to younger applicants, this might not be a problem. Perhaps you should focus on your strengths.

Option 5: This is an incorrect option. The opinions of your competitors aren't relevant to the success or failure of the rebranding decision.

Option 6: This is an incorrect option. You have to decide whether rebranding the company is the right decision first. Picking a marketing company assumes that it is.

Question

Match each visualization tool to its function.

Options:

A. Affinity diagram
B. 2 x 2 diagram
C. Flow chart
D. Mind map
E. Fishbone diagram

Targets:

1. Organizes hefty amounts of data into smaller, more

manageable themes or clusters
2. Compares options along two dimensions, such as cost and quality or risks and benefits
3. Outlines a sequence of logical steps and decision points, showing inputs and outputs, cause and effect
4. Develops ideas around a core topic and shows how the ideas relate to it and each other
5. Illustrates how various inputs correlate to produce an output

Answer

An affinity diagram helps organize large amounts of information and group them into common themes. It is most useful at the beginning of the critical thinking process when you want to find relationships between individual ideas upon which you can later expand.

A 2 x 2 diagram makes a visual representation of your thought processes so that you can compare two or more alternatives. For example, you might want to compare costs and benefits of two solutions.

A flow chart is especially suited for representing a solution where implementation will involve a step-by-step process.

A mind map is a representation of the ideas generated during a brainstorming session. With a core idea at the center, it uses shapes and colors to show groups of ideas and the associations and relationships between those ideas.

A fishbone diagram illustrates the various inputs or causes that have an effect on a problem or an issue. It is especially good for identifying the underlying reason a problem or issue has arisen.

Question

Due to high demand and sudden growth, you've decided to open a new branch to divide your company's work load.

When putting your action plan together, which questions should you address?

Options:

1. What outcome needs to be achieved to fulfill this business decision? 2. Who is responsible for overseeing the opening of the new branch? 3. When does the new branch need to be fully oper-

ational?
4. What work needs to be done and how should it be carried out?
5. What business problems will the new branch solve?
6. What alternatives should I consider if the new branch is unsuccessful? 7. How will opening a new branch further my personal career?

Answer

Option 1: *This is a correct option. The action plan needs to clearly state what the end goal is. That way you can stay focused on achieving the desired outcome.*

Option 2: *This is a correct option. An effective action plan must assign responsibilities to the people who will carry out the tasks involved in reaching the outcome.*

Option 3: *This is a correct option. The action plan must include a realistic schedule and indicate when the work needs to be completed. The available budget and manpower will need to be considered.*

Option 4: *This is a correct option. Explaining how the associated tasks must be carried out will also affect the schedule. The action plan needs to be detailed and specific so that everyone understands what must be done to achieve the overall objective.*

Option 5: *This is a correct option. The action plan needs to state what the motivation for taking action is. That way there's a direct correlation between the action plan and the context of the original issue.*

Option 6: *This is an incorrect option. The purpose of the action plan is to translate your conclusions into an achievable and measurable outcome. It shouldn't focus on alternative outcomes since these would need their own action plans.*

Option 7: *This is an incorrect option. The aim of the action plan is to serve the business by achieving the desired outcome: opening a successful new branch. It's not concerned with how the experience will benefit anyone on a personal level.*

www.ingramcontent.com/pod-product-compliance
Lightning Source LLC
Chambersburg PA
CBHW070857220526
45466CB00005B/2019